MOSTLY

ABOUT PRAYER

LETTERS
TO
JACOB

FR. JOHN-JULIAN, OJN

PARACLETE PRESS

BREWSTER, MASSACHUSETTS

2016 First Printing

Letters to Jacob: Mostly About Prayer

Copyright © 2016 by The Order of Julian of Norwich

ISBN 978-1-61261-686-5

All quotations from Holy Scripture are the author's own translations from the Hebrew and Greek originals.

The Paraclete Press name and logo (dove on cross) are trademarks of Paraclete Press, Inc.

Library of Congress Cataloging-in-Publication Data
John-Julian, Father, O.J.N.
  Letters to Jacob : mostly about prayer / Fr. John-Julian, OJN.
    pages cm
  ISBN 978-1-61261-686-5
  1. Prayer—Christianity. I. Title.
  BV210.3.J63 2015
  248.3'2—dc23   2015030191

10 9 8 7 6 5 4 3 2 1

Published by Paraclete Press
Brewster, Massachusetts
www.paracletepress.com
Printed in the United States of America

"Now you ask about my method of meditation. Strictly speaking I have a very simple way of prayer. It is centered entirely on attention to the presence of God and to His will and His love. . . . Yet it does not mean imaging anything or conceiving a precise image of God, for to my mind this would be a kind of idolatry. On the contrary, it is a matter of adoring him as invisible and infinitely beyond our comprehension. . . . [My ordinary way of prayer, or meditation] is not 'thinking about' anything, but a direct seeking of the face of the invisible, which cannot be found unless we become lost in him who is invisible."

—THOMAS MERTON[1]

I

*Y*ou know, giving spiritual advice by mail is a little like marriage by proxy—it is sometimes the only thing possible, but it is certainly the least desirable of all options. Ideally, I think, these sessions ought to involve exchange, questions and answers, experimentation, and the chance for me to sense intuitively what is going on with you spiritually, to hear not only what you *say* but the tone of voice in which you say it, and to pick up on your affective signals which are often more revealing than any amount of substance. But we are in a situation now where it is either by mail or not-at-all. So, we'll have to do the best we can with what we have.

I want to warn you ahead of time that you are going to hear a lot of personal views from me—often at loggerheads with popularly accepted opinion. But please be assured that these are not mere flights of fancy on my part or simply private preferences. I will do my best never to lay an opinion on you unless I can show you that it is backed by reason, common sense, and experience.

I promised to write to you about contemplative prayer—and I will—but I think there must be some considerable backfilling by way of addressing prayer more generally first—that is, to talk about what most people mean when they speak of prayer. So I think we will spend a little time in high school and college before we get to post-graduate work!

You already know that I believe firmly that most of what passes for personal prayer is so immature and undeveloped as to be either irrelevant or dangerous or both. By and large, the parish experience (which is how almost everyone encounters the Church) tends to train us almost exclusively in ethics. The majority of sermons or lectures one hears are about ethics/morality or theology. And serious ascetics—that is, deep concern about matters of prayer, meditation, and the spiritual life—are typically left on the back burner or, indeed, sometimes actually opposed or ridiculed.[2] As a result, the majority of Christians—even those who would be called "committed" and "active" are still praying (if at all) at a fairly immature level. Indeed, the very words they use (and their prayers are inevitably "said") are usually either those learned at their mother's knee or found in *The Book of Common Prayer* or on some Hallmark card! But "God is great and God is good" or "Now I lay me down to sleep" don't really pass muster as adult, responsible prayer.

But Christians can't be blamed for their ignorance because generally they have never been taught any better. (I heard recently from an honest layman who said, "Look, when I go into a church, I simply kneel down and count to sixty and then I sit in the pew—I don't know what else to do.")

But we really do need finally to ask the unpleasant question: when you speak those recurrent common words—"I will pray for you"—what do you mean? Usually those words mean something like, "I will ask God to make things better for you"—which has some odd implications because it seems to suggest that either God doesn't know what's best for you unless I tell him, or God has not been paying attention to you until I remind him, or God is more impressed by my words than by yours alone. (I know that I am being flippant here, but unless we face these implications, there's no point in talking about these things at all.)

That phrase—"I will pray for you"—*can* be redeemed. It *can* mean "I will declare to God that I stand in solidarity with you in your pain/trouble" or "I will be with you in your need" or "I will offer to you whatever grace I have" or even, possibly, "I will try spiritually to bear some of your pain myself." And I think you should notice that this kind of intercessory "praying" has more to do with my relationship with the *sufferer* than with God. It recognizes the human (and mystical) bond that exists between myself and the sufferer— that we are limbs of the same body, united both in joy and pain—and that my prayer simply recognizes and makes palpable what already exists.

So, you and I are going to do our best now to escape from the prayer trap. I'm going to ask you to suspend all other judgments and put your specific relationship with God on the front burner—ahead of service to others, liturgical prayer, theological study, the pursuit of virtue, penance for sin, and all such. I would point to Jesus's words in Matthew's Gospel: "Strive *first* for God's own realm and its righteousness, and *then* all other things will be given to you as well."[3] Later on you can sort out your priorities among those other things, but for now, and for our purposes, do me the favor of putting your prayer life—your life with God—in the very forefront.

$\mathcal{S}$o, I didn't scare you off yet, and you are game to go on.

All right, now we will get into some different (and difficult?) properties of prayer—that is, different from the way most folk understand it. Prayer which does nothing but ask God for something is, in one sense, simply futile—because it can have no effect whatsoever on the perfect God who is entirely changeless.

Admittedly, that's a subject that could fill several volumes of theology, but it points out the fact that the *way* we pray to God depends entirely on what we *believe* about God. And, as Michael Mayne put it: "If anyone ever gives you a clear and precise notion of who God is, you may be sure it is false."[4] God's very changelessness is part of that indescribability. Scripture agrees:

> The Lord spoke to Malachi: "I, the Lord, do not change. . . ."[5]
> The prophet Balaam said: "God is not a human . . . that he should change his mind."[6]

and the Church agrees:

> "Be present, O merciful God, and protect us through the hours of this night, so that we who are wearied

by the changes and chances of this life may rest in
your **eternal changelessness**; through Jesus Christ,
our Lord. Amen."[7]

I can tell you from my own experience that this idea of
God's changelessness takes some getting used to since our
habits of thought usually include a pretty anthropomorphic,
fairly primitive idea that God's mind can be changed by
human pleadings.

Our "asking" prayers must face up to the fact that time
itself was created by God and so God stands entirely *outside*
of created time, and we cannot, therefore, expect God to
change anything because of our prayer. So, if we intend to
offer a prayer of petition, we must realize ahead of time that
God will not be affected by that prayer of ours. But although
prayer doesn't change God, it can change you, the pray-er,
and that is extremely important.

To be appropriate, then, a prayer of petition must
always be conditional. Dame Julian of Norwich put it this
way: "Lord, Thou knowest what I wish—if it be Thy will
that I have it; and if it is not Thy will, good Lord, do not
be displeased, for I want nothing except what Thou wilt."[8]
You see, the daunting thing about the prayer of petition is
that one could conceivably be praying for something that is
directly *contrary to* God's own will! It is possible that one could
be blinded by the circumstances or skewed by the emotion

of the moment and actually be praying *against God!* Indeed,
we are so seldom absolutely certain that we *know* God's will
that our praying must always include a clear submission to
that divine will—whatever that might be. If one insists on
petitioning God, it must always be: "God, I want this—*but
only if it is what is your will.*" Our Lord modeled this for us in the
Garden of Gethsemane: "My Father, if it is possible, let this
cup pass from me; yet not what I want, but what you want."[9]

You can begin to see why I think it is spiritually wiser to
avoid praying for *any* specific outcome for one's self or others.
Certainly there may be a psychological benefit in expressing
one's hopes/wishes/desires in prayer—it's a way of "venting,"
of getting it off one's chest—but it is better that the heart of
the prayer always be the desire to see (and recognize) the
Will of God. The benefit of this kind of prayer falls mainly
to the one doing the praying—because it reinforces for the
pray-er the ultimate necessity of placing oneself (or one's
suffering friend) in God's hands, neither making demands
nor adding qualifications. This sense of prayer is clear in
Mother Julian's definition: "Prayer is a true, gracious, lasting
intention of the soul one-ed and made fast to the will of our
Lord by the sweet, secret working of the Holy Spirit."[10]

In addition, sometimes one's inclination to pray for
something may be a prod for one's own action. For instance,
I certainly cannot validly pray for a poor and needy person if
I am *doing* nothing to alleviate his or her condition. I cannot

pray for the lonely elderly person unless I am visiting her and providing her with some social options. And I cannot pray to pass an examination with flying colors unless I have done all the necessary study and preparation that are my responsibility to be ready for it.

I also want to share with you a practice that I have made my own: Simply stop asking God for anything! Instead of all those multiple prayers of petition, I simply think of prayer as nothing more than a conscious sharing of myself with God (as with a very dear friend) rather than making a request or entreaty. I do that by using what communication experts call "I-messages"—that is, verbally imparting to God my own condition/situation *without requesting any solution or correction*. For instance, such a prayer would be phrased something like: "I'm feeling worried about tomorrow's exam" rather than "O, God, help me pass the exam." I describe the problem in the prayer without asking for a resolution. This allows me to express my worries, feelings, and needs without making demands on God. (After all, God knows exactly what is best and will always do what is exactly right without anybody asking.) Contrary to popular bumper-sticker theology prayer does not change things—but it may change the one who prays. And I find I often add an affirmation to the message: "God, I'm nervous about starting my new job—but I know you are always with me."

There is also one common prayer that many of us use—although seldom with any deep consciousness of its implications. That is the prayer of thanksgiving. (Where I usually attend Mass, I smile when Form VI for the Prayers of the People is used, because they have dozens and dozens of names listed for "the special needs and concerns of this congregation" but when it comes to "We thank you, Lord, for all the blessings of this life," there is usually a long silence—only interrupted by the rare birthday. It seems that gratitude is not a very frequently practiced virtue.)

Real gratitude is merely the case of putting into words the recognition that everything we are and everything we have is from God's hand. But it is rare to hear anyone praying, "Thank you, God, for creating me." (In a recent Office we recited Psalm 139 with its great thirteenth verse: "I will thank you because I am marvelously made.") After all, my father and mother equipped me with a body, but it is God who has created my unique soul/mind/spirit/personhood. In a true sense, our parents make us organisms—but it is God who makes us humans. And gratitude to God for one's capabilities, aptitudes, and competencies is powerfully appropriate.

To offer thanks to God at table is fairly standard in Christian homes, but even as a ten-year-old I had a hard time understanding how God was responsible for that roast beef, those baked potatoes, and the green beans. I knew this food came from farmers and the markets and was cooked by my mother, and God's connection seemed tenuous at best (especially when it came to mackerel and broccoli—both of which were clearly invented by the devil). But then, a few years on, I ran into Maltbie Babock's verses:

> Back of the bread is the snowy flour;
> And back of the flour the mill.
> And back of the mill is the wheat and the shower,
> And the sun and the Father's will.

That's pretty juvenile and a bit sentimental, but at least it made poetic sense to my adolescent self. Of course, I was eventually able to break away from such elementary insights and recognize the gratitude owed to God for *everything*. But what I think we really need to avoid (and help children avoid) is the simplistic and even mechanistic idea that God planted seeds and harvested vegetables. Actually, what we should be thankful for is God's having devised this massively intricate and endlessly complicated universe that works so amazingly together to feed us, support us, and protect us.

I once wrote an academic paper on Julian's words *thanke* and *thankyng* in which I translated her definition with a more static and future-directed orientation: "Thanking is a steadfast, inner awareness, with great veneration and humble awe, which turns us with all our strength toward the deeds to which our good Lord guides us." For her, whenever we give thanks

the strength of our Lord's word
is directed into the soul,
and enlivens the heart,
and introduces it by his grace into true practices,
and causes it to pray most blessedly,
and truly to delight in our Lord.[11]

It's a wonderful idea to me that one's prayers of gratitude actually encourage and advance spiritual growth and cause improvement to happen. As the consciousness of one's indebtedness to God grows through prayers of gratitude, one's willingness to accept and embrace the whole will of God grows with it. And that's ultimately what human life on earth is all about.

P.S. Since you know my connection to the Order of Julian of Norwich, you will not be surprised when I refer to her ideas frequently in our correspondence—but don't blame the Order for any of this—the ideas are mine alone.

$\mathcal{Y}$es, that last letter did ask a lot of you—a lot of thought and also some challenges to the way you were used to thinking about things. I'm glad you took it between your teeth and didn't let go until you'd worked it out. As you wrote: "When one holds on to a difficult idea for a while, it becomes simpler and simpler." And, as I said, as you immerse yourself more and more in that mysterious idea of God's changelessness, all of your spirituality will begin to mature.

I know that next I want to talk about the prayer of penitence or repentance of sin, but I really can't allow myself to do that without talking a bit about sin itself. It is sad to say but ever since the early Middle Ages, the Church has by-and-large been neurotically obsessed with sin! The fact is, sin has been the Church's stock-in-trade, and without sin Christendom would never have become as powerful as it did. You see, first the Church invented hell. (I know that sounds strange, but there *was* no afterlife of horrendous pain and suffering for mortal sins in the Jewish tradition—only a pale, half-life in Sheol. Our idea of hell came from the Church—and from Jesus's references to Gehenna—Jerusalem's ever-smoldering town dump.) And one would be consigned to this hell of suffering because of mortal sins committed during one's lifetime on earth. [Note that even in considering hell, it seemed impossible to escape from the idea of time—that the afterlife was thought of as an endless passage of time, day after day after day, endlessly painful for sinners and endlessly joyful for saints. In fact, eternity is *not* "a long, endless time"—eternity is ***no time at all***—it is beyond time altogether—like God.]

Originally, it seems that the very early church considered four sins to be mortal—apostasy, rape/adultery, murder, and theft—and for those she provided for public confession, a long period of penance (now called "Lent"), and final absolution and restoration to the community ("Easter"). But over the centuries the Church adjusted and altered the list of mortal (or "deadly") sins, finally settling on seven: pride, lust, gluttony, greed, wrath, anger, and envy. And the practice of any of these was enough to consign one to hell.

Now, I ask you, do you know anyone who has not committed one or more of these sins? Of course not, because that was the idea: if fairly common sins could cast one into hell, how could anyone be saved? Well, the Church—and the Church alone—held the answer: the Church's bishops and priests could absolve you of all your sins and save you from hell. That's something no other power on earth could do. So, for over a thousand years the Church held the keys to heaven and hell. And dozens of religious orders were founded and hundreds of abbeys, minsters, and cathedrals constructed all across Europe as visible evidence of penance for sins. Sin became a huge, moneymaking business for the Church, and she made the best of it. As a result, sin loomed menacingly and darkly over just about everything that was called Christian. Look, for instance, at this first prayer of confession in English from the 1552 *Book of Common Prayer* and *still* published in the present Episcopal Prayer Book.[12] I'll leave the old spelling to show you its age.

> ALMIGHTIE God, father of our Lorde Jesus Christe, maker of all thyngs, Judge of all men, we acknowledge and bewayle oure manyfolde synnes and wyckednes, whiche we from tyme to tyme moste grevously have committed, by thoughte, woord and dede, agaynst thy devine Majestie: provokyng most justely thy wrath and indignacion agaynste us: we doe earnestlye repente, and be hartely sory for these our misdoynges: the remembraunce of them is grievouse unto us, the burthen of them is intollerable: have mercye upon us, have mercye upon us, moste mercifull father, for thy sonne oure Lorde Jesus Chrystes sake: forgeve us all that is past, and graunt that we maye ever here after serve and please thee, in newnesse of lyfe, to the honoure and glory of thy name: Through Jesus Christe our Lorde.

I have always wanted to ask Archbishop Cranmer, the author: is one supposed seriously to believe that our measly little sins provoke "[God's] ***wrath and indignation*** against us"? Wrath and indignation? That's more anthropomorphism than I care to handle. (I much prefer Julian's thirteenth chapter: ". . . in God can be no wrath. . . .") And is the burden of our sins truly "grievous" and "intolerable" as the prayer says? Well, they must have been *somewhat* tolerable, since these words of confession in the Eucharist were originally used in church only four times a year, so one's sins—grievous though they may have been—were apparently *fairly* tolerable—at least for three months' duration.

But the difficulty today is that it seems one is inclined either to accept this over-emphasized prominence of sin or to embrace the opposite extreme in which such a thing as sin doesn't exist. The middle (and reasonable) line is that sin is certainly a *serious issue*—because it is a matter of choosing *against* God and opposing God's will and love—but behind and beyond it we have the absolute, total, universal forgiveness of all sins for all people by the crucified Lord. Sin is an ulcer on the Christian soul, but its forgiveness has already been won; forgiveness already lives within the sinful soul and merely waits to be liberated and activated by repentance. Mother Julian, in her typically insightful way, put it thus: "To the soul this was a mighty wonder . . . that our Lord God, as far as he is concerned, cannot forgive—because he cannot be angry—it would be impossible."[13] For this enlightened lady, God has not the least animosity toward sinners; indeed, he *pities* sinners rather than judging them. God has already forgiven them—2,000 years ago! And so God's forgiveness lies right smack there, ready to be picked up at any time by any repentant sinner.

One last note on sin: there is an unfortunate phrase in the confession in Prayers of the People Form VI in *The Book of Common Prayer*.[14] It is ". . . forgive us our sins, known and unknown. . . ." The problem is that classical moral theology has always held that in order to be a sin, an act or thought must always be *intentionally sinful*—that is, the sinner must *believe* that what she or he is about do is a sin and then choose to do it anyway. "Unknown sin" suggests that there is some objective reality out there that is *always* sin—and that is not so. You cannot sin unless you actively choose to do what you consider to be sin. The point here is that *intention* is the first essential ingredient for human sin. One cannot sin "by mistake" or without knowing it. (For a first-century Jew, on the other hand, sins were simply a list of six hundred and thirteen particular forbidden acts—and one was guilty of sin if one committed one of those acts—even though one did not intend to err, did not know he was doing it, and meant only to do right.)

For instance: it is a clear, sunny day, I am well-rested and entirely alert, driving down a city street at about twenty miles an hour when suddenly a little boy dashes out from between the parked cars and my car hits him and kills him.

Now I have just murdered someone—but I am not guilty of any sin at all, because I had no intention of harming him—indeed, I had every intention of *not* harming him or anyone, and I had done all that was reasonably possible to avoid causing harm. (Even the secular law recognizes this distinction and would not charge me for murder.) But, you see, there are so many intricate, complicated, and complex dimensions to discerning sin that by-and-large one ought to be strict with oneself, but avoid making any judgments about anyone else. Again, Julian is wonderful: ". . . for the beholding of other men's sins makes, as it were, a thick mist before the eye of the soul, and we cannot for the time see the fairness of God. . . ."[15]

What then, does all this say about the prayer of repentance? Well, I think there are two important aspects to that prayer: first, we must stop the cringing, groveling, and pleading for forgiveness—as though it were something God granted only grudgingly or resentfully. Our repentance must truly be sincere, honest, and sorrowful, but real repentance is rather like backfilling—that is, we already know the outcome before we start. We *know* we are forgiven the moment our repentance is genuine. So our responsibility is to be as deeply *sincere* in our penitence as possible—not because it wins us any favor, but because it discloses the integrity of our contrition. And without that integrity or sincerity the forgiveness remains obscured.

Second, the function of our prayer of repentance takes some practice because it is notably different from what we are used to. It is not so much a begging for forgiveness as a recognition and declaration of our own failure and weakness—and the reminder that we are already mystically inhabited by an ever-forgiving God. (". . . God *lives in us* and his love is made complete in us"[16] and ". . . that we may evermore dwell in him, *and he in us.*"[17]) To my mind, the primary dimension of true penitence is that of humility—that the acknowledgment of our sin is the recognition of our own deficiency or foolishness. So let our penitential prayer be genuinely self-judging and let it demonstrate our dependence on God who alone makes us whole.

And, one cannot leave the subject without mentioning reparation. If my sin has caused any harm to others, then part of my prayer must be the "making good" of that harm whenever possible. If something has been stolen, it must be returned or recompense made. If someone has been hurt, there must be apology, repair, and true remorse. This is, as it were, the *human* aspect of the process of atonement: to undo—to whatever degree possible—any harm we may have caused. Again, primarily an experience of humility!

Finally, as I said above, in its earliest years the Church provided for public confession, reparation, and absolution of the four major sins. But then in later years, word leaked out that in the monasteries, the monks were allowed to make *private* confessions to their abbot and obtain absolution. And finally the pressure from the laity got to be so great that the Church had to change its practices—and private (auricular, i.e., "in the ear") confession had to be made available to all. It is still there—though used probably too seldom. But when your sin is an especially serious and somber matter about which you feel substantial guilt, you may wish to make use of the Sacrament of Reconciliation by making your confession to a priest, and receiving the guarantee of absolution. This is particularly valuable at significant turning points in one's life: baptism, confirmation, matrimony, ordination, before life-threatening surgery, and the like. How to choose a confessor? Easy: just ask the priest if she or he makes their own confession! One who confesses makes the best confessor.

*T*hat was an awful lot of ascetical theology to squeeze into that last letter, but I think misunderstanding about sin and forgiveness is a major problem for Christians today—with many religionists unwilling to let go of the dark, judgmental dynamics of sin and accusing progressive Christians of ignoring sin altogether. Don't try to swallow it all at once—take it slowly and a little at a time. There's no hurry.

Now I want to introduce you to a fifth kind of prayer that may be the most rare (and possibly the most fundamental) of all verbal prayer, even though you may never have heard it named. It is what our *Book of Common Prayer* calls "The prayer of oblation." This is truly the act of the sacrifice of self—of the offering of oneself on the altar of God's will—and it is poetically summed up in a single Hebrew word: *hineni*—which means, quite simply, "Here I am." We first encounter it in the book of the Genesis (22:1): "After these things, God tested Abraham. He said to him, 'Abraham!' And he said, 'Here I am.'" And later (46:2): "God spoke to Israel in visions of the night, and said, 'Jacob.' And [Jacob] said, 'Here I am.'" And again in the book of the Exodus (3:4): "God called to him out of the [burning] bush, 'Moses, Moses!' And [Moses] said, 'Here I am.'" The same words appear in the first book of the prophet Samuel (3:4): "Then the Lord called, 'Samuel!

Samuel!' and [Samuel] said, 'Here I am.'" And finally in Isaiah's sixth chapter: "Then I heard the voice of the Lord saying, 'Whom shall I send, and who will go for us?' And I said, 'Here am I; send me.'"

It's nearly ubiquitous among the prophets, and obviously, *hineni* is much more than merely a personal locator. If we were to translate its actual meaning, it would be much more significant—perhaps something like, "I stand here, ready to serve and to obey you, my God." Or "I am at your beck and call." And that, in its simplest form, is the prayer of oblation— the true offering of oneself (with no strings attached) to God to be used wholly to work God's will. It appears most graphically in the solemn life vows of a monk or nun in which the candidate offers all one's possessions, one's body, and one's will to the service of God and God's children. In that monastic world, this is often called "vocation," but vocation is God's calling of *every* Christian—and not just to an obviously and overtly monastic life. It takes a deep commitment for one to put oneself literally in the hands of God, ready to undertake whatsoever God seems to be asking—because what oblation truly is, is a serious commitment to a life of uncompromised and authentic virtue. Indeed, following God's will is a perfect definition of what virtue is. But it takes a very deep faith to listen profoundly and vulnerably to God's whispered direction. (God never seems to speak aloud anymore—except when using someone else's voice.)

God's will is to be exercised not only in the life-changing moments, but just as often in the more diminutive matters— when to go to bed, and when to rise; what to read next; whether one should accept the new job offer in Oregon; which church one should attend; and the like.

The prime substance of the prayer of oblation is the diminution of one's own willfulness and the increasing submission to the will of God. But the most wonderful thing about the prayer of oblation is that the more one practices it, ever so gradually that Divine Will becomes more and more plain—indeed, eventually one no longer even needs to *ask*, because God's will is patently present and becomes apparent so that one's submission to it becomes literally habitual. One practices virtue without even thinking about it. (The masters often differentiate between "acts of virtue" which we commit intentionally and by choice, and "virtuous acts" which we do simply by habit without even thinking about it.) So the prayer of oblation is surely an anti-ego devotional practice— and therefore, by the way, a fine preparation for the practice of contemplative prayer.

I only caution you not to get hung up on God's "silence." In fact, God is *constantly* revealing the Divine Will to all of us at every second of every minute of every day, but it is seldom obvious, and the subtleties seem sometimes to be inscrutable. If you are experiencing a "silence" from God in your prayer of oblation, the grand solution is simply to wait—indeed, just such amenable waiting may be precisely what God wills at the moment and in itself can lead to serious spiritual growth. Imagine an entire spiritual lifetime spent doing nothing except waiting for God! Few of us will ever have dramatic divine epiphanies or booming voices from heaven, but many of us may spend our days blessedly waiting for God.

When I founded our Order, I developed a four-part axiom—a touchstone, as it were—regarding our life of prayer: Await, Allow, Accept, Attend.

Await: no one can rush God! God knows exactly what one needs and when one needs it. Indeed, God knows us better than we know ourselves. And sometimes our greatest unperceived need may be simply for patience, serenity, and quiet readiness.

Allow: God is who God is—and God is *not* who you or I think God might be. We must simply forsake our expectations of what God is like because *all* of them are wrong and inadequate. God will define his own divinity—and we will never wholly understand it.

Accept: Once we concede that God is neither recognizable by us nor predictable, we must be ready to accept whatever manifestation (or lack thereof) God may choose.

Attend: We must develop the habit of paying attention to every aspect of present reality because God is revealing the Divine Self to us at every moment in unimaginable and scarcely conceivable ways—in our hearing someone else's words, in the pages of a book we may be reading, in some natural phenomenon, in an unusual and unpredictable insight. (In Zen, they call this "mindfulness.") We need to recognize that our minds are both the home of our free will *and* God's primary door into our lives. God simply cannot and will not compromise our free will by "making" us do anything (to do so would be to rescind our humanity), but God *can* urge, suggest, hint at, or remind us of possibilities for the exercise of virtue, and we need to learn to be sensitive to such subtle divine inspiration.

I have always been troubled by the prayer "O Lord, make us have perpetual love and reverence for your holy Name . . ."[18]—because if the Lord "makes" us have perpetual love, then it is no love at all because it is not freely chosen. I have always wished the prayer said: "O Lord, *help* us to have perpetual love. . . ."

An overarching goal of all our prayer—of whatever form—must then ultimately be the ceaseless search for the will of God, and final submission to that will when or where or how it is revealed.

$\mathcal{S}$o you noticed that lying hidden behind all our varied styles of praying is actually the single goal: the discernment and embrace of God's will and making it our own—to paraphrase Danielle Nussberger: "a selfless reorientation to the Other."[19] That's right. And one smiles at all the complicated theological stew that people have made of that incredibly simple construct.

For a little variety (and as we approach the boundary line between verbal and nonverbal prayer) we should think a bit about the two components of prayer usually called "the prayer of praise" and "the prayer of adoration."

"Praise the Lord" is a familiar phrase to those in the Charismatic tradition—along with "Amen" it is the familiar retort to a salient point made by a preacher. But praise is not only appropriate in such a circumstance. It ought to become an integral part of *all* our experiences of prayer.

I have often defined praise as "bragging to God about Godself." In fact, it is little more than the gratifying recognition of God's true glory—reminding ourselves of the grandeur and awesomeness of God which is beyond our comprehension or expression. It is a good antidote to the inclination to think of God as "cuddly"—it is the compensating recognition that the little baby Jesus in the lowly manger is *also* the gleaming Christ of the Transfiguration, that the maternal God who gathers us under her divine wings is also the God who rides across the firmament on the awesome winged leonine cherubim. As is often the case in Christian undertakings, we are called here simply to pay attention to what actually IS—to honor a dimension of reality that we too often take for granted and too easily overlook. And it is good to remember that some of the greatest works of art and music in history have been devoted to just that praise of God. (For example, there are one hundred and sixty-one hymns in the Episcopal hymnal section labeled "Praise to God.")

When all is said and done and every prayer has been prayed, we are finally driven beyond the elegant language and high-flown intentions to fall in the utter silence of adoration before the God who is beyond all—invisible, immeasurable, infinite. "Let all mortal flesh keep silence" indeed. Veneration is the real conclusion of all prayer in which we are the actors, the doers. Worship is what you and I were made for—it is the fulfillment of our human nature to adore our God—whom Julian calls our Maker, our Keeper, and our everlasting Lover, and our endless Joy and Bliss.[20]

This is a relatively short letter because there is little more to say about the adoration of God: What we discern in adoration is God's majesty: a beauty we cannot imagine, a love we cannot conceive, a truth beyond knowing, an unimaginable splendor, and a perfection that outreaches our farthest understanding. And yet this adoration is one of the simplest of all acts of prayer—simply gazing in wonder on God. As the holy St. John Vianney put it when asked how he spent so much time each day kneeling before the Blessed Sacrament: "I gaze on Him and He gazes on me."[21]

That brings us to the end of thinking about the kinds of prayer in which we, the pray-ers, provide the input—prayer that is mostly our words, our thoughts, or our actions directed toward God.

VI

*N*ow we cross the first of the two great internal borderlines that fall within the far-reaching territories of prayer. We move to a prayer in which, while there are certainly things we *do*, we have a primary orientation toward *what God wishes to reveal to us*—toward discovering what God is showing us or telling us, often in obscurity. I have called this "still prayer," since in all its manifestations our own stillness is its most significant dimension.

Just as our prayer so far has been addressing God, now we concentrate more on *listening* to God, on perceiving what God wishes to communicate to us. In its broadest terms (as we will use the language here) this is called "meditation." (You will hear the term "discursive meditation" used to describe this activity, but that suggests "conversation" and I think that is misleading.)

In fact, there are dozens of set methods of meditation—ascribed to saints and spiritual masters and the like—most of which claim to be "the one proper method." As one who has meditated and done contemplative prayer daily for over thirty years, believe me I know the territory, and I'm going to write to you not according to anyone's famous guaranteed method, but on the basis of my own experience. In your letter, you express concern that you do it "right"—but I want to ask that you listen to what I have learned from my experience, and if it makes sense, follow it.

First, I find that receptive meditation (a better label!) can be verbal or written, as well as nonverbal or oriented around an object. For some people, meditation works best when it originates in a written text—Scripture or a holy writing of some kind. Others find it works best for them if they concentrate on some object—icon or crucifix or something else.

The verbal approach is quite simple: it means taking a few lines of Holy Scripture or a few lines from the writings of classical masters such as Thomas Kempis, Francis de Sales, John of the Cross or of modern guides such as Thomas Merton, Richard Rohr, or James Finley—or even a phrase or two from a familiar liturgy. You read that passage and re-read it perhaps six or seven times—and then you simply give your mind over to move freely among those words, hopeful that your attention may be drawn to something of value that may be hidden there, or something that others have tended to overlook, or some insight that is particularly relevant to you at that moment in time. This is usually called *lectio divina*. Most people translate that over-simply as "divine reading." I prefer "heavenly learning."

The important element here is to develop such deep familiarity with the passage that the Holy Spirit is able to lead you through the thick undergrowth of ordinary comprehension into the open plain of profound insight—

something that wasn't previously noticed, and possibly, a perception tailored specifically for you at that very moment. It is also entirely possible that your meditation time may bear no noticeable results at all—that there will appear to be only silence on God's part. Don't be fooled by this apparent silence. Let yourself be satisfied with nothing more than your own willingness to be open to God—and understand that what God is working in you may be imperceptible at that point and only recognizable in future retrospection.

The other way to do much the same thing is to use an image, an icon, or a statue as your point of entrance. Proceed much as in the heavenly lesson above. Let's say it is an icon: stare at the icon, gaze on it, focus all your attention on it. Look at every tiny bit of its detail. Then (here's the hard part), move into it and through it to a reality that is hidden within and behind it. The down-to-earth and literalist traditions of Western culture are so strong and so technically pragmatic that it is usually difficult for us to allow ourselves to pass beyond the literal image into the deeper Realities behind. We are too willing to settle for the obvious when the image or icon should really be seen as only a window into a celestial authenticity. (Note: that is why you will not see *true* icons with lifelike figures and perspective. They are meant to represent something *beyond the ordinary*, so the usual real-life, naturalistic depiction is avoided in favor of traditional, stylistic figures and poses. No saint ever actually *looked like* his or her icon—intentionally.)

And here is where we'd better clarify the difference between kataphatic and apophatic prayer. So far, we have been dealing only with kataphatic prayer—that is, prayer that uses words, images, symbols, thoughts, and ideas—measurable, quantifiable material and forms. Gazing at a crucifix, contemplating an icon, absorbing a fragment of the Gospel, using rosary beads, reflecting on the life of a particular saint—all these are kataphatic because they use some matter outside oneself.

On the other hand, apophatic prayer is a more passive experience in which one tries to separate from any and all external matter, clearing the mind of all specific ideas, thoughts, or images and avoiding any specific expectation or result—asking nothing, saying nothing, beholding nothing, thinking of nothing, anticipating nothing, demanding nothing. The goal is to avoid anything that smacks of attention to or gratification of the ego in order to make oneself vulnerable to God—which is, after all, the ultimate purpose for which we were created. Apophatic prayer is a prayer concerned with *being* rather than *doing*, with *availability* rather than *activity*, with inhibition of the self in order to make a more unobstructed space for God. For years our religious order has used Maggie Ross's term "still prayer" to describe this experience,[22] since the very essence of this prayer is ***inaction***.

This is just to whet your appetite! I'll deal more thoroughly with still prayer in the next letter!

VII

I think you already know that I am convinced that if one undertakes a serious, long-term, intentional program of prayer, one will inevitably be led in the direction of contemplative prayer. I don't mean that one ignores or rejects the more elementary approaches, but as one matures spiritually one tends to become more familiar with God, as it were. So the tendency is to begin to think of prayer more as just *being with God* and *offering oneself* rather than bemoaning one's sins or trying to coax God into doing something. "Still prayer" is a *state* rather than an *action*, and is, in fact, the prayer of the soul and the prayer of heaven. It is the mode of prayer that is truly eternal and will never in all eternity disappear.

I admit, I'm a bit of a cheerleader for the contemplative way (that's an awkward metaphor, isn't it?), and yet I certainly don't mean to say that other kinds of prayer have no place in one's life. But they tend more often to be preparatory or developmental functions *on the way* to something deeper. If the goal of prayer (like the goal of all humanity) is perfect union with God, then movement in the direction of the contemplative is really essential and ought not to be thought of as esoteric, enigmatic, or arcane, but as a principal pathway.

So here we pass the second borderline—between productive, receptive meditation, and true contemplative prayer.

The mystical tradition of the *via negativa* ("the negative way") basically holds that the limited human mind can know nothing about God directly, except what God is NOT. For example, since we have never experienced eternity it means nothing to say that God is "eternal"; however we can accurately say that God is *not* temporal). A similar approach can be used in considering contemplative prayer—i.e., we can speak about what contemplative prayer is NOT—but I would rather discuss it in terms of what I have come to think of as the stages, or steps, that must be passed and transcended as one moves toward developing skills in the work of contemplative prayer.

Most everyone, in the beginning, enters these stages or steps and, experiencing the ascetical *poverty* of them, abandons them. For too many people, when that sense of failure comes, it means the end of their contemplative effort. When it stops "feeling good," when "nothing is happening," when "God is absent," the tendency is to drop it. As a spiritual advisor, I counsel the exact opposite: that this "collapse" is often the ***single most hopeful and positive sign that a person is growing in prayer***. It is when prayer stops "feeling good" or meeting our expectations that we can begin to suspect that possibly, just possibly, the Holy Spirit may have begun to pray within us, and we may be just beginning to approach what I extravagantly call "deep prayer."

I do not present these just as things to avoid. All of them are impediments to true prayer, but for us fallen human beings it is almost impossible to approach prayer without one or more (or all) of these elements being present to some degree in the early stages of our growth. Consequently, when we sense that we are experiencing one, and that it is beginning to fail us, that is precisely the time to hold on, to remain absolutely faithful, to refuse rejection, and then to pass through the experience, leaving it behind, for the next one.

In theater, there is something called a "scrim"—a gauzy curtain that is hung across the stage. When light is shined on it from the front, it appears to be simply a backdrop or a wall, and action can take place in front of it. But when the front lighting is turned off, and the stage is lit *behind* the scrim, one can see right through it. Each of these stages is something like a scrim. If attention is paid to it, and we are acting out our prayer in front of it, it will seem like a wall. And when we experience failure, there will be a sense of hopelessness, and that is the time when, by the grace of God (or at the suggestion of a spiritual advisor), we can raise our spiritual eyes and take another, deeper look—and see that what we perceived to be a wall is actually only a gauzy veil. We can pass through it into the mystical reality it previously masked.

If we are deeply faithful, these hindrances will all eventually be stripped away, and we will recognize true prayer in its own inexpressible, unembellished, uncloaked mystical beauty.

I should also add here that instead of something to be avoided, most of these veils are actually *promoted* as goals by certain contemporary "schools" of prayer—notably those that are inheritors of the Wesleys' idea that all true prayer is "heartfelt," and those that promulgate a "charismatic" or "Pentecostal" approach to prayer. Some of these are Old Testament ideas that are frequently promulgated by biblical fundamentalism. Please don't think it overly severe for me to discourage what others are promoting, but I have seen real horrors promulgated in the name of contemplative prayer (and spiritual lives harmed) that I feel it is important to name these demons in order to expurgate them. But all of that background is enough for now. Next time, I'll dive headfirst into the problems that face a novice contemplative. But first, send me some sort of response to all of this, will you? And let me know how it strikes you.

VIII

$\mathcal{T}$he first veil that impedes the development of still prayer is the **emotions.** In eighteenth-century England, the Church of England was at the lowest ebb it has ever reached. It was more ghastly than modern Anglicans can imagine: there were no altars as we know them—only tables which most of the time were used to hold coats and canes and umbrellas. Churches were filthy, vestments (beyond the black-and-white of surplice and tippet) nonexistent, candles were considered Romish, and crosses were seen as papist. The entire mystical and ceremonial tradition was ignored, and the parish church looked and acted like little more than a very dull book-reviewing society. Religious "enthusiasm" was looked down upon condescendingly and sneered at, and true "churchliness" was despised.

Into this musty morass came the brothers John and Charles Wesley—both "high church" Anglican priests. John, who was very much affected by a Moravian friend, experienced an emotional conversion experience in 1738 and went on to preach and teach the importance of such experiences, and an emotional and "heartfelt" approach to religion and prayer. He was hoping to bring some vitality and life to the tedious, dull Church of England. His ideas eventually came to influence virtually all of Western Christendom, and although he would have deplored it, tended to sidestep churchliness and equate emotional experience with mysticism and spirituality.

There is hardly a Christian in the West today who does not equate true prayer with "feelings." The problem with this is that there is nothing less dependable in this world than human emotions, and it proves to be exhausting and ultimately impossible to maintain peak emotions on anything like a regular basis—so "prayer gushes" are sought as often as possible, and between them one depends on memories of the past "gush" or expectations of a future one.

An emotion-based spirituality is also utterly *self*-oriented, and individual personal emotional satisfaction becomes its entire criterion and goal. It is a concept of prayer that is almost wholly confined to the this-worldly emotional experience, and, since it defines the God-experience completely in temporal and somatic terms, it effectively closes off the experience of transcendence. It limits God's actions to those that can be perceived bodily and emotively.

This is not to say that the highest contemplative experiences may not upon occasion have emotional components—trances and raptures, even—but that those components are in no way a criterion for the validity of the prayer. In fact, following the guidelines of the great mystics, one can reliably determine that continuing emotional consolations are virtually always an indication of a rudimentary and undeveloped (and sometimes dangerous) spirituality. Sometimes God provides such consolations for those who are beginning the Way as encouragements and support for the effort. But when one begins to move into serious contemplative commitment those consolations are *always* withdrawn. Indeed, **the *absence* of emotional consolation is most frequently a sign of spiritual growth and development**—as God withdraws the easy and the sentimental in favor of the true. So the inclination to judge the validity of prayer by the quality of its emotional components—by "how it makes me feel"—is superficial and puerile. In any serious spiritual growth, one must pass through the emotional dimensions and leave them behind, neither requiring nor desiring them. As Julian says in discussing the less attractive experiences of prayer: "And thus, it is in our feeling, our foolishness, that the cause of our weakness lies."[23]

I know it sounds strange to think of prayer as feeling-less, but in the long run, this is the only "safe" kind of praying—because it is the only kind we can rely on with any sort of permanence. And it might be good to remind ourselves that heaven itself is beyond earthly experience, so even heavenly joy ought not to be understood as a kind of upgraded earthly happiness—it is beyond our comprehension.

Let me add one last metaphor. When I was a parish priest and used to do premarital counseling, I told the couple that eventually the time would come to all couples when they will sit down at the breakfast table, look across at their spouse and think, "Why in the world did I ever marry *that*?" In most cases, that moment is considered the end of the marriage—but, in fact, it is the very *beginning* of real married life—because one's reply to that awkward question is: "It doesn't matter *why* I married my spouse, because the fact is that I *did* marry her/him and now we need to begin the real job of making this marriage work." (In fact, this liberation from the mild lunacy of being "in love" is an excellent opportunity to build a reasonable, genuine, and fruitful life together.) So it is with prayer—when prayer stops "feeling good" (as it *always* will) that is the point where *real* praying begins.

But enough! Let that idea soak in your mind and heart for a bit.

IX

You mentioned in your last letter that you are having difficulty "processing" some of what I have been saying. I did warn you that this wouldn't be easy or smooth. I often ask people: "If you love God when you're wealthy and the sun is shining, how do you feel about God when the tornado hits and the stock market crashes?"

So, we take a look now at the second impediment—closely related to the first. It is plain and simple **boredom** and dullness, springing often from repetitiveness, discipline, and the absence of novelty or innovation. Boredom in prayer is like boredom in marriage—it is an irreplaceable and essential ingredient that allows you to come eventually to the point of making the final decision in favor of *faithfulness* without being swayed by the criterion of emotional satisfaction.

Boredom is a prime tool God uses to lead us from the emotions of the body to the reason of the mind and from there to the intuition of the spirit. In a world in which pleasure is almost always something "done to us," there is an expectation that God will entertain us in our spiritual lives, making spirituality fun (like watching TV). The modern Christian joy enthusiasts know nothing of the classical, quiet, faith-based, deep, still, and *true* joy of the contemplative that springs from the ever-faithful acceptance of sameness, dullness, and drabness. As Julian writes: ". . . frequently our trust is not complete, for we are not certain that God hears us, because of our unworthiness (as it seems to us) and because we feel absolutely nothing, for we are frequently as barren and dry after our prayers as we were before."[24] A goal of serious prayer cannot be the selfish seeking of "kicks" or "goodies."

In his book on classical fairy tales,[25] Bruno Bettelheim wrote that by and large, those traditional tales are not "moral stories," but that there is one aspect of moral character universally promoted and praised in all of them: the simple virtue of faithfulness. And the older I get, the more I believe that this is the core virtue of true prayer—a virtue that ignores all aspects of the empirical experience in favor of consistency and utter dependability. It is only when one makes a relentless and unswervingly concrete commitment to prayer that it becomes possible for God to begin to act significantly in that person's life. When I hear someone say, "I recite Morning Prayer several times a week as often as I can fit it in," my inclination is to say, forget it. The Office (like the rest of spiritual discipline) cannot do its true work without *absolute and unwavering reliability*—otherwise, it's no more than a minor spiritual blip. And this discipline is the only way I know of getting through the veil of boredom (or any of the other veils).

This is why I often recommend that folk begin with a very small commitment and be *totally* faithful to that commitment—ten minutes of still prayer every morning *without fail* is worth immeasurably more than two hours "whenever you can find time for it."

It is the exercise of this virtue of faithfulness that guarantees the space in which God can work—a work that is *always* quietly cumulative, seldom frenzied, or immediately volatile. The fact is that the last person to know if one is making any headway in spirituality is oneself. It happens so slowly and subtly that you can recognize spiritual growth only years afterward in retrospect. I remember John Henry Newman's words: "We shall not perceive ourselves changing. It will be like the unfolding the leaves in spring. You do not see them grow; you cannot, by watching, detect it. But every day, as it passes, has done something for them; and you are able, perhaps every morning to say that they are more advanced than yesterday. So it is with our souls; not indeed every morning, but at certain periods, we are able to see that we are more alive and religious than we were, though during the interval we were not conscious that we were advancing."[26]

So don't worry about attempting to measure any of this. In fact, avoid all measurement. Just be faithful—regardless of anything!

*Y*es, I realize that you are feeling as though most of the props have been knocked out of your prayer life—but, believe me, there is a lot more. The third veil that must be bypassed is **activity**. We live in a "can-do" culture, and usually one of the first questions we hear about prayer is: "Well, now, what am I supposed to do?" My response is usually, nothing! Indeed, if you wish to grow in true prayer, you must resist the temptation to "do" anything, and learn to stop whatever it is that you are already doing. There is a very real sense in which true prayer is something *God does* to, with, and within the soul that has been emptied, is vulnerable, and waiting. It is not one's own activity—no matter how urgent or well meant—that validates prayer. As Moses told the Israelites: ". . . you need only keep still."[27]

And yet the "doing nothing" which is so essential and central to mature prayer is one of the hardest assignments we of this twenty-first century can have. To stop the mad dash of our lives and wild clatter of our minds is extremely difficult. Just waiting on God seems unproductive and so frustrating. And yet, even *The Book of Common Prayer* defines prayer as "responding to God"[28]—that means waiting on God and on God's time and on God's will. I might paraphrase the insight of Giacomo Leopardi:

"Human beings can get used to anything—except doing nothing."[29]

The real secret is the discovery and development of a process resulting in vulnerability and availability to God. This means that we must find a way to divert and detour all our usual worldly concerns and activities and considerations. We must really put them away from us and divorce ourselves from them. Just as "leisure time" is an essential in artistic creation, so it is an essential in deep prayer. One cannot do true still prayer while keeping a hand in four different projects at the same time. The only kind of activity that can be conducive to still prayer is a repetitive, mindless one that does not require attention (e.g., you can do still prayer while stirring the soup, but not while concocting the recipe; you can do still prayer while repeating a meaningless mantra, but not while doing an intricate exegesis). It is interesting that the author of the mystical *Cloud of Unknowing* describes this process as putting all earthly matters under a "cloud of forgetting."[30]

The fact is that God is ready and willing to help us make ourselves unconditionally available, and our serious wish to be quietly available will be supported and aided by God. But this requires discipline. It means arranging a time and place where we can be as undisturbed by other aspects of our lives as possible. A "prayer corner" is a good idea, if it is separated from the main highways and byways of your life. Even the anchorite in her cell usually had an "altar" as a focus for the life of prayer.

But, you know, a major component of serious prayer is the realization (as the mystics remind us) that *true* prayer is not prayed by us but by God-within-us. Our primary task, then, is to get our egos, our "selves," out of the way. Check out Romans 8:26—"the Spirit unites himself with us in our weakness; for we do not know how to pray as we ought, but the Spirit himself intercedes for us with inexpressible sighs." I know that that old saw—"Let go and let God"—is a bit of a cliché, but it is ultimately a good formula for beginning contemplatives. The idea is to get out of the way and stop worrying about methods or returns on our investment.

The fourth encumbrance is that of our own **expectations** of who God is and how God works. First-century Jews were visited by the Messiah they had hoped for and expected for over 800 years, by the incarnate Son of their Yahweh God—and yet, except for a handful, most missed the visitation because they were *looking for something else* in a Messiah. They wanted a prince, a ruler, and a general of the armies who would free them from the oppression of Roman occupation. They saw liberation in a purely this-worldly, political light, and so, when Christ came and brought them the offer of ultimate and mystical liberation, they missed it.

We suffer from a social conditioning by our parents, our teachers, and our church to think of an encounter with God in a certain way. We have come to expect that such an encounter will always be "warm," for instance, and "hope-filled" and "rewarding." It will always be "positive" and bring "joy" and "peace." Consequently, if a particular spiritual practice or discipline does *not* produce these expected results, we trash it and declare it useless. All because God is not meeting our expectations.

As I wrote in an earlier letter, in our Order we have a fourfold adage that guides our life and our prayer: Await, Allow, Accept, Attend. We structure our prayer life so that we can **wait** for God, and so that we can **allow** God to manifest the Divine Self or not, just as God chooses. The simple phrase is "Let God be God," rather than demanding that God conform to our private ideas about him. (By the way, even the use of the male pronouns in referring to God is loaded with limiting expectations. What if "he" wishes to manifest "his" femininity?)

But that means that whatever happens in our praying may be immeasurably beyond anything we could ever have anticipated. It even means that pain and anguish may be the result of our praying rather than comfort and ease—that God may reveal some divine aspects we never expected.

And then, having awaited God's pleasure, and allowed God to be who God is, we can **accept** whatever God sends us, and we can **pay attention** to whatever that is, rather than tapping our foot impatiently waiting for God to meet our own expectations.

I often hear from beginners: "I spend half an hour in still prayer and I only experience the *absence* of God." I reply with theology: "Is God actually absent? Of course not! So God must have decided that you are now spiritually able to be shown a divine dimension you never knew about before—a dimension of God's being that *you* have called 'absence.'"

XII

$\mathcal{I}$ know that you are still surprised at the number of potholes that seem to blight the road to God. Perhaps you are discovering how difficult it is to steer around them (or to get out, once you have gotten stuck). The smooth pathway offered by our Sunday school lessons is truly a fiction. I'd say that Good Friday is often the appropriate classroom for the beginner.

But, as we continue to grow, the fifth veil is **obscurity.** We need to transcend the obstacle of seeing God as separate from and extrinsic to us. This almost universal failing has come about because of the loss of most of what is mystical in the ordinary life of a Christian in a parish church, and because our tendency is to see God as another oversized, invisible human being.

After all, our only usual experience of relating to another person is the relation we have with another human being, and so when we think of relating to God or Christ, we think of it in the same manner because we are unaware of any other options. Any other human being I relate to is always (a) other than me, (b) separated from me, (c) at some distance from me, (d) dependent upon what I say to get to know me. So we are inclined to think of and to approach God in the same way. We think of God as a separate person/being, off at a distance from us, needing us to communicate so he can know what's going on. (Or at least we think of him as a kind of magician who can know from a distance by some mystical monitor what we are doing or thinking—a kind of celestial mind-reader.)

Thus we find multitudes of books on spirituality that describe the "journey to God" or the "pilgrimage to Christ." We often speak comfortably about our own "spiritual journey" but if the word *journey* means "going from one place to another place," there is no such thing as a "spiritual journey to God," and all of the books one can read on that subject are simply wrong.

In the early church, Christ was understood to be in heaven (and therefore immediately available to everyone) and/or in the assembled church (notably at the Eucharist). In both cases, his Presence was mystical, not governed by the laws of physics. But by the late Middle Ages, Christ came to be primarily thought of as an individual human person who died in terrible pain on a cross in Jerusalem in the year AD 30, and who was present in some incomprehensible way inside the consecrated Communion Host of the altar. In both cases, Christ's presence became linked to something *visible*—the Body on the cross, the Host in the tabernacle. Christ got "located" and locked in. Gradually the idea of a mystical and all-pervasive presence of Christ almost died out (or was labeled sneeringly as "panentheism").

That is the legacy we inherit today! And that is why we talk now as though Christ were somewhere else, separated from us, a long distance away, or in some other era of history. That is simply a falsehood.

Christ's presence is and (since the Resurrection) has always been a mystical presence—and a mystical presence does not take up space *anywhere*. The mystical presence of Christ is right here—we Christians are surrounded, enwrapped, immersed in, and indwelt by Christ—and we have been so at least since our baptism. There isn't any place to go where we can find Christ any more fully than we can find him right here. Indeed, speaking of going on a journey to find Christ is like a fish going on a journey to find the ocean. We are surrounded by, immersed in, and drowning in Christ; therefore our so-called "journey" must be an effort to remove the blinders and veils from our eyes, to open our souls to recognize and be aware of Christ/God around us and within us and everywhere.

We also speak of "following Jesus," but (unless by that we mean that we mystically go to the cross with him) that, too, seems a worldly concept. One "follows" a great teacher, but one *lives within* Christ. Christ is not just some great man who gave us a valuable set of rules about how to live a good life—which rules we should obey. Christ did not come to make us better people; Christ came to reincorporate us into himself (and therefore directly into the Holy Trinity).

Christ's concern is not with *behavior* but with *being*, not with *activity* but with *ontology*. We are about as separate from Christ as a bird is separate from the air beneath its wings. Try to recognize this intrinsic character of your life *within* him. There is no wall or distance that separates us from Christ; there is only our refusal to see him and to recognize him and to experience him as he is. As Thomas Merton said (paraphrasing St. Augustine): "God is not someone else."[31] And as Paul writes, quoting Deuteronomy: "The word is near you: on your tongue and in your heart."[32]

Related to this problem is our tendency to think that this "separation" from Christ/God is something we need to overcome—like a task assigned to us if we want to be near God. It is as though God purposely distances himself and then gives us the job of traversing this distance in order to get to him. But the opposite is true! It is *God* who is seeking *us*. We are the objects of God's search; we are the sought! It is we who frustrate God's wish and intention to be in perfect union. It is we who erect barriers and interject the distance. It is we who by our own actions—often by our "religious" actions—keep that same seeking God at arm's length. Indeed, the union with him that God wishes for us to recognize is more often than not frustrated by us *in the very name of religion*. The medieval Church particularly elevated God to an obscure and immeasurably glorious distance—so utterly different as to be virtually unapproachable (except of course, by the august ordained). The Church took God away from the people, and perched God on an inaccessible throne, and only the mystics reminded us of God's immanence in creation and in our souls.

XIII

$\mathcal{Y}$ou mention that we never seem to stop to rest, but are always moving. As J.R.R. Tolkien put it in his Hobbits' walking song: "The road goes ever on and on" and as one moves toward the goal of true prayer, the next veil encountered is that of **methodology**—a real bugaboo.

In any one of a thousand religious bookstores, you'll find a dozen books on how to meditate and how to do contemplative prayer. Each author touts his or her own method or means as the guaranteed method. You will find intricate directions about how to breathe, how to position the body, what time of day (or night) to pray, what mantras to use and how, what procedures to follow, words to say, exercises to undertake, objects to gaze upon, and what to think or not think. Even the best masters whom I sincerely respect tend to be trapped in the snares of methodology. (I recently read a fine short booklet on contemplative prayer in which the monastic author debunked the "methodology craze" and declared that there was no "proper" method . . . except, of course, how one breathed.)

One of the very great things about following the spirituality of Dame Julian is that in no place in her book does she even faintly suggest a "method" for praying, or a "method" for living a prayerful life. She gives us her own insights into the nature of God, the nature of humankind, and the quality of our relationship, but (aside from stressing the importance of the sacraments) she suggests no specific procedures.

Does one really think one can learn how to make love by adhering to a sex handbook? Does one really propose to become a violin virtuoso by studying an instruction manual? Surely, it does no harm to know how others may have done it, but it *can* do great harm to think one must do it in the same way. Contemplative prayer is, quite simply, *the natural state of the soul*. It is the condition for which God created the soul and equipped it perfectly for that function. What one must do is simply to *stop*—thinking, planning, expecting, organizing, even wondering.

One can gaze on an icon or a crucifix or a tree or the ocean or a floorboard or a flyspeck on the wall—or one can close one's eyes and gaze at nothing. One can use a constant mantra (repeating some phrase or word endlessly) or an occasional mantra (concentrating on a word only when distracted)—or no mantra at all. Use a rosary or Jesus Prayer beads or a knotted cord or a cross between one's fingers— or nothing at all. Stand or sit or kneel or lie down or walk or slouch in a chair. (The finest contemplative I ever knew usually prayed either prone on the floor or settled into an overstuffed armchair.) Do still prayer at night, at dawn, at midday, or at twilight. Go to a church or chapel or a personal shrine, your bedroom, outdoors, or wherever you are. Use the Ignatian Method, the Sulpician Method, or the Augustinian Method, or any other—or no method at all.

Please take my word for this because I don't know anyone else who says it plainly. The goal of still prayer is quiet centeredness and availability to God, and *whatever* produces that state for an individual is appropriate and right for that individual.

You are probably not old enough to remember the fascinating (albeit very pre-Vatican II) novel *Brother Petroc's Return*[33]—about a sixteenth-century Benedictine monk who comes alive in a twentieth-century monastery and is driven to the brink of a nervous breakdown by the complicated methodology of prayer demanded of the monks. Finally, with the help of a wise old monk, he comes to the realization, "You mean, all this is just supposed to bring one closer to God? Oh, I live with God all the time!"

I do not mean to suggest that there is no methodology of contemplative prayer, but I do mean to indicate that there is no *one right method*. I also do not mean to suggest that one ought not to read and study all sorts of methodologies— it is often a great help to learn how some earlier and holy, proficient masters practiced still prayer—as long as you realize that such study is *informative*, not *prescriptive*. You will find your own way finally by letting go of plans, projects, and catalogs of methods and allowing God to lead the way.

*Y*es, I know that setting off on this sea of prayer without a predetermined map is a frightening challenge, but don't forget this: the seventh shroud impeding true prayer is **ignorance**—ignorance of the true nature of God and the true nature of humankind. Certainly it is true, as any great mystic will readily vouch, that one can never know God in any complete or definitive way by means of the intellect. It is also true, however, that ignorance of basic theology can send you on a fruitless search for God in all the wrong places and in all the wrong directions.

Unfortunately, we live now in an age of almost universal theological illiteracy. To say nothing of the laity, most of our clergy (supposedly trained in theological discourse) do not even have at their command an adequate language in which to discuss serious theology. Empiricism and existentialism (which place the individual at the center of the universe, with all reality depending for its very existence upon his/her perceptions and experiences) have become the theological norms of our individualistic and self-absorbed age—and, within the constructs of those theological frameworks, mysticism is a literal impossibility.

It is no wonder that in the sacrament-denying traditions, there is really no such thing as a classic mystic. Mysticism (and its handmaid, the contemplative way) requires a sacramental and incarnational theology—whether it be Augustinian (i.e., Platonic) or Thomistic (i.e., Aristotelian) in tradition. That is to say, we must operate on the basis of a theology that places Reality beyond the reach of normal perception, but which links it to that-which-is-perceived in some essential way. This means that the "experience" of God is not and cannot be an end in itself—since that "experience" for us earth-bound creatures is virtually always emotive and affective (or, what Thomists would call "passive," i.e., originating in the passions).

We need to understand God as something other than "a big, invisible human being." We must understand (as far as we can) the implications of pure spirituality itself. We must grapple with comprehending (or, better, intuiting) God's timelessness, unchangeable constancy, total independence of us, utter ubiquity, and the absence in God of any accidental or existential attributes. We must wrestle with the emotionally unrewarding comprehensions of what I call the "affective thinness" of Divine Nature. (God's own being is more like the frail, delicacy of the manna than the rich, rewarding opulence of the flesh-pots—it sustains, but without sensuous gratification.)

We must struggle with the incomprehensible mystery of the oneness of the Trinity (which describes not only God's nature, but our own)—the substantial bond existing within a community that is of such a nature that the community may be described with equal validity as a single unity.

We must contend with the false projection of human anger and wrath onto God, and the unredeemed primitive ideas of God as a "punisher." We must come to know that God's "judgment" is not some extrinsic evaluation laid upon us, but an always-accurate perception and revelation of exactly what, where, and who we are.

We must comprehend the idea that ultimate and divine Love, Truth, Beauty, and Goodness have absolutely nothing to do with "feeling"—indeed that God does not (and cannot) "feel" anything at all, and that the divine mandate to us to love, follow the truth, honor beauty, and cultivate goodness is not a call to us to "feel" anything, either.

And before we can pray well, we must also seek an orthodox comprehension not only of God, but of our human selves, both our limitations and our glories. We must fly in the face both of the Calvinistic, Puritan condemnation of humanity with its ideas of "total depravity," as well as the hedonistic humanism that deifies the entire human reality. We must come to know that we are truly perfectible *and* that we are truly sinners at one and the same time. Virtually all the mystics say that we carry within ourselves a "splinter" of God—an "image," a "spark," a "godly will," an "ember," a "shard" which is itself divine; and virtually all also say that we are "nothingness" and that we must deny or "naught" ourselves if we are ever to rediscover our oneness with God: that is one of the multiple paradoxes we encounter in still prayer. We must recognize that in creation God planned and prepared humanity specifically to share in divinity—in the Trinity itself—and that there must, then, either be something of "the divine" in our nature or we could only adhere (like some alien and foreign barnacle) to the "outside" of God and never be able to come to coinhere within the Holy Trinity. But we are fools if we forget that as human beings we are also inevitably sinners, seeking by repentance the universal gift of forgiveness.

XV

I know that was a lot to chew on, in my last letter. Take your time with it. There is no need to rush. I am hoping that you will return to these ideas several times, reading what I have written over and over, as you deepen your prayer practice.

But for now, let me press on to the next veil that encumbers contemplative life. It is a guilty **consciousness of sin.** Sin is, of course, a central issue in any serious prayer—but it is not a very important issue. Yes, you read that sentence correctly! Mother Julian on several occasions counsels that we not pay much attention to sin, that we not allow it to take over our consciousness, that we not absorb ourselves with it. She wrote, "[Sin] has no manner of essence,"[34] and ". . . my sin shall not hinder His goodness from working"[35]—because we must remember that God and the Church know exactly what to do with sin: they forgive it! And the forgiveness that is offered is already present—indeed, has been present for almost 2,000 years. It is no question of whether or not God will forgive our sins (that has already been done!), but only a question of whether or not *we* will choose to accept and assent to that already-available forgiveness.

It usually seems to be fun to sin, and in our twisted culture it also seems paradoxically desirable to go on wallowing in self-accusing guilt about our sins. It is certainly not the *sins* that impede our unity with God, but our absorption with the *guilt* of those sins. One of the devious by-ways of the "righteous" is to encourage dwelling on our sinfulness. Such introspection is blindly egotistical, and effectively God-expelling. It is only our ignorance of the true nature of God, and our repudiation of Christ's already-accomplished redemptive act, that can make us so consumed with consciousness of our sins.

Sin is dealt with simply: it is recognized (never excused!) and then offered to God for forgiveness. If it is of particular gravity or particularly upsetting, then one has recourse to the Sacrament of Reconciliation. That is that! (I know I wrote about some of this before under the prayer of repentance, but it bears repetition.)

There is not, and can never be, a "battle" between goodness and sin, God and the Devil—the two are of completely separate orders of being, and sin, evil, and wickedness are utterly and completely impotent in the face of God. You and I may tend to give the Devil a great deal more power than he has (and it does please Satan when we do that) but in and of himself, he is next to nothing. Julian helps us to see that Christ's reaction to the Devil is to *scorn* him[36]—to ignore him, to overlook him, to pay no attention to him, to turn our back on him and not give him the credit of any notice. He is a large zero—only a big hole in creation—and we should treat him as such.[37]

Mother Julian declares that *sin hath no maner of substance.*[38] It is not a "thing," it is merely the absence of goodness—a vacuum in the atmosphere of God, a blank spot on the canvas of the Creator Artist, a dark absence of the Light. It is no-thing, and flies from God as darkness flies at daybreak. All that needs to be done with sin is that it be brought out into that Light and it evaporates. Expose sin to God and it is gone! Sin is like a paper cup in a museum case of golden chalices—it is not worth the attention we give it. It is transient and irrelevant and should be merely looked at, acknowledged, repented, and discarded, not allowed to taint our souls thereafter.

XVI

$\mathcal{S}$o, you discovered my tendency to hyperbole in my last letter! Of course, sin ought not to be *ignored*, but it ought not to be over-hyped, either, which is the point I wanted to make.

And the next veil we need to bypass in order to come to mature still prayer is that of **romance**.

In her splendid (posthumously published) book *The Poetry of Search and the Poetry of Statement*,[39] Dorothy Sayers provides a valuable definition of, and distinction between, classical and romantic art. Classical art, she says, is art that is oriented toward its end, goal, purpose, statement, and message. Romantic art, on the other hand, concerns itself mainly with the *process* of getting wherever one is going, with the *feelings* one has on the way, with the experience of moving through a process, and the goal is irrelevant. Classical art is goal-oriented; romantic art is process-oriented. (I recently heard an actor speak about styles of acting: he said, "In 'modern' acting, one gets into the character and merely goes with the flow; in 'classical' acting, one has a clear map in one's head about where one wishes to go with the character." It is the same distinction.)

In that sense, still prayer is "classical" prayer in that one's only concern is with the goal and end of prayer, i.e., union with God. The feelings and the means and the methodology are all only servants to the end and goal and unless they lead to that goal they are irrelevant. I can always say to a serious student of prayer, for instance, "Forget about 'how to do it' and concentrate on God—then God will take over and lead you to do whatever you need to do. In still prayer, God is the 'doer' and we are only 'reactors.'"

There is another and more modern sense of the word *romantic*, however, which is also an impediment to still prayer. *Fervent, ardent, impassioned, torrid, tender, moving, touching, devoted, enamored* are all synonyms for this sense of the word—and they can all be found sprinkled liberally on the covers of romantic novels and many (most?) contemporary religious books. This kind of romance is simply a pretense, a fantasy, a delusion, and in prayer it can be a major obstacle between God and ourselves. The sentimental mushiness that passes for spirituality today (in virtually *all* "Christian" camps) is not only ascetically neutral or simply in bad taste, but an actual impediment to spiritual growth. Holman Hunt's "The Light of the World" or Elliott's "Just As I Am Without One Plea" or Pedro de Mena's "Ecce Homo" will always lead people *away* from Christ, not toward him—guiding them into their own sentimentality or pitiable fantasies, and away from the reality that is the Incarnate Lord.

The fact is that serious spirituality is a drag and a drudge and a bore and a pain, with not a single "romantic" thing about it.

In a monastery, monastics have to deal with this problem constantly in postulants who come to join the order. They come with the Gothic idea of monasticism—that it is all dark hoods and veils, rising sacrificially and nobly in the dark before dawn, the quiet swishing of long habits on flagstone floors, the glowing of candles in the dark church, and the ethereal soaring of Gregorian chant. Before long novices learn, however, that it is more often a matter of cleaning toilets and washing dishes and studying dull theology and tolerating Brother George's flat notes in choir.

If one comes to any spirituality or mysticism with this romantic notion, it will soon be destroyed—but, for too many, the spirituality will be destroyed along with it, and they will give up. There is not even one tiny thing about still prayer that is romantically satisfying. And to know that ahead of time should help.

$\mathcal{I}$ hope my debunking of romance was not too severe for you. I know that I tend to be a pretty stern taskmaster.

But I need to tell you about another aspect of this romantic veil: the mistaken notion of spiritual **privacy**.

Still prayer is *the most personal experience a human being can have*—and also *the most corporate and communal.* That said, it is never "private." Until one has been able to junk the idea that prayer is one's own individual spiritual pipeline to God, one will get nowhere in mature spirituality or in still prayer. There is only one way to relate to God, and that is from *within the Body of God's Son*— and there are no private corners in that Body. A "one-ing" with Christ means always a "one-ing" with the saints and angels and all of one's fellow Christians as well, so that if one's spirituality carries one off on a deviated, separated path, one can be assured it is not of God!

Your every prayer is automatically and properly a prayer of intercession—that is, if you are mystically integrated with the whole Body of Christ, then whatever successes you experience in perfecting that unity will benefit the whole Body (and similarly, your failures will degrade the whole Body).

Finally, perhaps the greatest danger for a mystic is solitariness. We were created by the Father within the community of humanity. Remember: Adam couldn't make it alone, and we are redeemed by the Son within the community of the Church (it was the *community* of the Apostles that experienced Pentecost). Our own spirituality must always test itself against the spirituality of that ecclesial community. Only then can one's private myopia be overcome, and one's tendency to private error be corrected. So, for instance, the presence of an experienced and accomplished spiritual advisor is a significant element in protecting against just such private illusion and deception. (I hate that term *spiritual director*—it sounds like someone conducting an orchestra!)

The doctrine of the Holy Trinity itself is repudiation for all time of the idea of "privacy" in spirituality. Our very God is a permanent and unrelieved Community! At the center of all Christian spiritual life is the *corporate* act of the Holy Eucharist (which ought to be a clear hint that "Holy Communion" is not an exclusive and private event). The plural pronoun that begins the Nicene Creed (i.e., *"We* believe . . .") is a clue that even our doctrinal faith is not private. Indeed, virtually all sin and error in the Church's history can be understood as the assertion of individualism and privacy over the communal and corporate. (The word "heresy" itself has its origins in the Greek *haíreo* that means literally "to take for oneself.")

So, although most often still prayer is practiced in solitude, away from other human beings, it does not and must not *exclude* them. You need to think of yourself as one of a multitude of mini-corks that keep the whole Body afloat.

You know, of course, that I who write these words am a hermit—a solitary. I live alone in a hermitage, and I leave my rooms only to attend Mass and buy groceries. And, indeed, many (most?) of the contemplatives we know from history were also solitaries. But we are solitary only in the narrow earthly sense. The uncompromised center of a hermit's spirituality must be her or his core sense of incorporation in the Body of Christ and union with the wider Church. That is why St. Benedict rules that a monk may have permission to live as a hermit only after many years of living in community.

I have this simple vision of someone going off to a mountaintop and whispering, "Finally, O God, I am all alone with you." and God's whispering back, "Well, I don't know about you, but there is a whole crowd of us here." It is that kind of "crowded solitude" that is the ideal.

$\mathscr{S}$ince we are human beings and live in a world in which our only ordinary experience of other rational beings is that of our fellow humans, and since we are all immersed in time and most of us have no encounters that can liberate us from the bonds of that experience, another veil we need to discard in still prayer is that of **projection**—that is, of seeing God and thinking of God only in human terms.

It is this projection of what we know of this world onto God that produces for us such concepts as a God who gets angry or punishes people, or a God who can change his mind or can be changed by us, or that we can make a deal with God, or bribe God, or that there are things we can do or say which will manipulate God into doing what we want. Since we only have earthly experience to go on, we haven't the slightest idea of how to relate to a Being, a Person, who is not human, and so we tend to project earthly humanity onto God.

I know some of this is repetitious, but it is deserving of repetition. Perhaps the hardest thing for us to understand is God's pure and unqualified supra-human spirituality— spirituality without extension or passion, without location or sentiment. Since union with this kind of God is the goal and end of contemplative prayer, it is easy to see why such a goal is unattractive to steamy, emotional, sentimental, modern humanity. For a culture that showers its highest adulation and attention on movie stars, football players, heavy metal rock, and crack cocaine, the idea of fulfillment, satisfaction, and joy on a *non-earthly* plane is virtually inconceivable. And today's evangelists are only too happy to produce a pop version of Christian "spirich'ality" which manifests itself in country-western hymns, *son et lumière* extravaganzas, sobbing penitents at the mercy seat, rainbows, unicorns and balloons. (They easily forget that the rainbow is the battle bow of a vengeful Yahweh hung in the clouds; that the unicorn is the symbol of a Christ who is captured and killed because he came vulnerably into the lap of a virgin; and that the balloon is only a toy version of one of the greatest war machines of its day.)

We smile today at the fantasies of a medieval world that projected earthly suffering into hell and purgatory; we nod condescendingly at the Muslim idea of hedonistic delights in the afterlife; but we do the same thing in our thinking about God and matters spiritual. We suffer either the mechanicalism of the Soviet astronauts who said triumphantly that they found no evidence of God when they got into outer space— or the sentimentality that thinks God is cruel for allowing dear Aunt Lily to die—or the sorcery of parents who care nothing for the Church, but always get their babies baptized so they won't go to hell—or even the theological technicians who oversee a Council of the Church in its efforts to define God down to the last divine toenail.

All of this is our effort to cut God down to size—to make God manageable and understandable on purely earthly terms—the terms with which we are familiar. And we forget that ". . . my thoughts are not your thoughts, nor are your ways my ways, says the Lord. For as the heavens are higher than the earth, so are my ways higher than your ways and my thoughts than your thoughts."[40]

In still prayer, we need to recognize that *anything* we know or think or can say about God is flawed and is either woefully inadequate or wholly in error, and if we spend our time looking for the God we have defined by earthly projections, we will miss the Divine Reality entirely.

As I've said before, one of the most important aspects of the contemplative way is the willingness to allow God to be whoever God is, not who *we think* God is. And that means that any close experience of God is going to be of so *unique* in nature, so far from anything we have *ever* experienced up to that point, that we run a real danger of missing it altogether because of our projections. (I remember as a Deacon taking Communion to a nun who had been in a coma for two years and had just awakened. She received the host, smiled broadly, said, "Oh, you will be so surprised!" and died.)

We call God "Father," but that does not suggest that God uses the men's room, or that God impregnated our mother, or that God is the ideal "daddy" none of us ever had; we say that God loves us, but that doesn't mean God "feels" anything at all toward us (since God has no feelings); we speak of Christ as being born as a child in Bethlehem, but that doesn't mean he abandoned heaven for Palestine, pawned his divinity for thirty years, and became just one of the guys; we speak of the kingdom, but forget that it has no castle, no throne, no knights in armor, and a monarch crowned not with gold but with thorns.

The fact is that too many of us (even some "good Christians") would find heaven so alien, so foreign, so unfamiliar, so far from anything we have ever known or dreamed, that we would not be interested in remaining there—and would probably not be interested in its King either—if we experienced God as God truly is. We flee from silence; we flee from solitude; we flee from purity; and we flee from sacrifice—all of which are definitive and mystical means of union with God.

God is not like us—*except* that divine mind is like ours (or, more correctly, we have a mind that is derived from and an image of God's). So even the unconscious ways in which we ascribe human characteristics to God are impediments to our growth. It were well we kept in mind: "No one has seen the Father except he who is from God, he alone sees the Father."[41]

As I'm sure you are noticing, there is a close connection among all these veils. Closely related to the veils of ignorance and projection is the veil of **literalness**. This is a very sad spiritual outlook that exploded on the American religious scene in the nineteenth century and in the multiplying fundamentalist sects of our day. It reads the Bible as though it were a science textbook. A literal interpretation of Holy Scripture is a major impediment to any serious search for one's unity with God, because it replaces the indefinable with the verbal, the ineffable with the obvious, and the inconceivable with the historical. It claims exhaustive and definitive truth for what is meant to be no more than a glimmer, a hint, at best a whisper of divinity.

No one (including God) can define God! No one can draw a line around God and say, "Here God is!" It is only one who is willing to let loose of all such earthly moorings and drift apparently aimlessly into the inconceivable mystical sea of ineffability who can ever hope to touch the Reality that one will still even then be unable to describe or define.

St. John of the Cross, quite simply, knew God. And all he could say about that was a very long collection of poetry.[42] Any honest truth about God will never fit into prose—even biblical prose! It is beyond ordinary (even inspired) words to describe, and must never be chained, bound, or restrained to the black-and-white marks any humans make on any pages—even scriptural ones.

This is surely one of the most difficult of basic understandings—that we will never understand or comprehend God this side of heaven. Even our standard definitions tend to be crippled and flawed: "God is love"— but it is such an unselfish, unfulfilling, unrewarding, non-emotional love that it is unparalleled in any of our experience, utterly *unlike* earthly love. "God is good"—but the divine goodness has no *moral* implications at all; there is no sense here of good "as the opposite of bad." God is good only in the same sense that the orbiting of planets around a star is good or the rising of sun at dawn. "God is great"—except that, for instance, the New Oxford American Dictionary carries seventeen meanings for "great," none of which adequately describe God.

We must finally be driven to admit that God is a complete and unknown enigmatic mystery—recognized only by those rare few to whom God has revealed himself—and even that is such that those who have lived through that experience cannot even describe it. It is beyond expression in words— except in poetry. (It's always been an impish temptation of mine to ask someone to describe God, knowing that the more they have to say, the less do they know God.)

We're nearing the end, now, and I realize that there is indeed one more veil.

The last veil we need to part is the veil that controls and orders the whole of current American life (no wonder we easily become slaves to its ways): **practicality**. If mature still prayer is anything, it is completely and utterly *useless*.

It produces no practical product and has no utilitarian values whatsoever.

It is a total waste of time and energy according to our culture's current understandings and values.

I smiled at a recent note from a British friend commenting that in England contemplative religious orders are not exempt from taxes—because they produce no "socially useful product"! And I recognize that the $3.5 million in secular grants that I obtained the last year before I became a monk are utterly unavailable to me now—grants are not given to contemplative religious orders—because contemplative religious orders are "useless." (Remember Thomas Merton's wonderful poem about the supposed "uselessness" of pine needles? Look it up!)

Unfortunately, American Christians tend to find this impracticality intolerable—and so they work very hard to convert their religion into some useful and productive activity. Religion is defined, then, as social services, or inexpensive therapy, or "spiritual healing." Even an atheistic dunderhead would have to see that there must be *something* to religion—if he can get his bunions removed miraculously, or if the churches keep homeless people off the streets, or if he can get emotional reassurance in counseling with his minister. There are some thriving Christian congregations in which, strictly speaking, there has been no attention paid to religion or spirituality in years.

So our still prayer is of no "use" at all. It doesn't heal illness or comfort the troubled heart. It doesn't salve the conscience or strengthen the moral sensitivities. It doesn't help people in need or bring peace to the world. All that happens in still prayer is that one does what God made human beings to do—and one becomes more and more what God intended human beings to be—one with God! That's all. And all the rest of it is up to God.

XXI

$\mathcal{O}$ne last personal insight of mine: you probably didn't notice it, but if one takes all those cautions and wraps them together, they are actually a rehearsal for eternity—they encourage the changelessness and oneness with God that is characteristic of heaven. In other words, a serious prayer life is an effort to allow heaven to come into being on earth. Of course, it's a mild watercolor version of the unspeakable brilliance of heaven, but the condition of true prayer is like an elementary imitation of celestial reality.

And now I am going to take you on one last, rare, fleeting dash across what I see as the last borderline in this wide world of prayer that I've been describing. It is almost exactly like the contemplative still prayer we've been talking about—in fact, I don't know any spiritual writers who would commonly make a distinction between the two, but in my experience, there is a difference—an almost indescribable one, but a difference, nonetheless.

It is simply this: the still prayer I have called "meditation" in its simplest form is nothing more than an attempt to make oneself *accessible* to God—willing to hear what God might convey, or act as God might direct. In other words, meditation really means waiting upon God—open, vulnerable, focused, susceptible, listening, and ready. In meditation, one tries to be passive and willing to be communicated with. It is a great pinnacle of spiritual life and devout experience.

But there can be one step more, and I gather here the wisdom of two anonymous sources: the sixth-century author writing under the name of Dionysius the Areopagite and the fourteenth-century nameless author of *The Cloud of Unknowing*.

It is this: that when one has detached oneself from every earthly entity and even from consciousness of self, one is not immediately filled with an awareness of God's own presence. One has removed the obstacles between the self and God, and is as open as possible to God's guidance, God's intervention, and God's aid, but one is not actually seeking a bond with Godself.

That is the difference.

There are some people—few in number—who may practice still prayer assiduously and faithfully, love God genuinely and follow Christ, live exemplary virtuous and unselfish lives, and still feel mildly or oddly incomplete or unfinished, stirred in their intuition to "something more." These are the few whom God calls to the ultimate event of human life—to the momentary experience of perfect unity with the invisible, unknowable essence that is God.

First, I must be very clear that this is an utterly unique vocation, given to very few. It is not available to the general public, nor something one can earn or learn. In all my many years, I have known only one person with this calling, so I pass this on to you with tremendous caution because it is exceedingly improbable that you are so called—but I want you to know of it so you can recognize it if by any long chance you ever encounter it in yourself or in another.

In this case, following the master of *The Cloud*, I can only describe it from a distance. Here it is: one has literally put away everything of the earth and all self-consciousness and every expectation of God or what God may be like—all of that put away as dead beneath a "cloud of forgetting" (as our guide puts it)—and knowing nothing more, turning away from all else, encounter in one's mind the cloud of unknowing that covers and hides the indefinable Divinity, the *Deus Absconditus*, the hidden no-thingness that is God. And without consciousness of it, acting only on inspired instinct, one selflessly casts at that concealing cloud the utmost gift one has to give—the "nakid intent": what our *Cloud* master calls the "lance of longing love."

However, it must be said that following this stringent pattern, one may lay love-laden siege to that hidden cloud of divinity for an entire lifetime without a single deeper awareness. Or conceivably in a rare, singular possibility one may be gifted with an instantaneous, momentary, immeasurable searing flash of the Inexpressible Reality—and nothing will ever be the same again.

Now, do not, my beloved son, expect this to happen—but know (as I do) that there have been those who have experienced it. One can say that mystically it is a kind of imitation of the process of dying and discovering heaven while still alive on earth. (When I think about it, I seem always to hear the voice of dying Saint Stephen: "I see the heavens opened. . .,"[43]) And I am reminded of the centrality of both death and undefeated life for much of Christian belief and practice: the death and new life of Holy Baptism; the celebration of the death and resurrection of Christ in the Eucharist; and the death and transformation of self in still prayer.

Further, remember that there is nothing in the world you can do by yourself to *attain* this experience unless you are stirred: it is a special and unique calling from God, unearned by those few who receive it, and unavailable to those who are not specifically called to it by God. But at least you can know that it is there. . . .

XXII

$\mathcal{N}$ow I want to send this last letter because I have been trying for weeks to think of a metaphor for prayer in general that takes into consideration all the many approaches we've talked about. Let me try this:

Time, in this metaphor, is a circular, moving river— occasionally rushing rapidly between narrow banks, and then widening and flowing slowly at other places. All human beings are afloat in this river of time, and are being rushed along by the river around and around the circle of time. Along the bank of the river is a great granite outcropping with a deep cave in its midst. That granite cliff is the timeless, changeless God of the metaphor.

Most people simply sweep right past this divine Crag without taking any notice of it at all. Their attention is entirely absorbed with the river itself, where it is going, whether their boat is secure, and what is around the next bend.

Then there are those who seem to be somewhat aware of the Rock Face, and they notice it as they rush past, but they have no thought of diverting from their course.

Others may have a deeper awareness of the Cliff, and they pay such serious attention that when they reach that point, they actually slow down their craft, as they gaze at the Stone.

There are yet others who are so aware of the Mount that they can bring their boat almost to a stop, and reach out and touch the Stone as they glide slowly past.

And there are those who—although they don't fully understand the matter—slow down their vessel, forget their previous goal, and step out of the river of time. They scale the mount and stand at the top for a time—and they often do this repeatedly after they have returned to the river.

Finally, there is a mere handful of people who stop their craft and emerge from the river, let their boat go, climb the Pinnacle, discover the cave, and settle themselves there to remain forever.

My dear son, I wish you the best of luck in all your mountaineering, and I leave you with these words of Thomas Merton:

> . . . [H]ere we seek the naked presence of God in apparent nothingness. If only we find Him, the emptiness becomes perfectly full, and the contradictions vanish. But in order to do this we must be faithful to a will that is inscrutable, which does not reveal itself in simple and clear-cut decisions as we would like to think.[44]

In God,

John-Julian, OJN

AFTERWORD

This book began—as its title suggests—as a collection of some thirteen letters of advice to a young seminarian who was newly interested in ascetical theology and particularly in experimenting with contemplative prayer. The letters were originally written in the late 1990s, and have been revised and rewritten, edited and expanded, emended and adapted at least a dozen times since—and even, for a time, were promulgated in pirated copies among a few seminarians and were required reading in at least one seminary class in ascetical theology. They have never been formally published before, and for this book they have been extensively edited and amplified.

All of the content, ideas, opinions, advice, and practices in this book are, of course, my own and do not necessarily reflect those of the Order of Julian of Norwich of which I am a hermit Member Regular. All quotations from Holy Scripture are my own translation from the Hebrew and Greek originals, and since the original letters did not have footnotes, I have inserted citations as endnotes. I should also add that there are a number of repetitious passages that I have retained since they seem harmless and can only help to remind the reader.

I have tried very hard to avoid using gender-specific pronouns and using masculine pronouns for God, but occasionally there is just no reasonable grammatical way out!

John-Julian, OJN

NOTES

1 *Hidden Ground of Love;* (Shannon, William H., ed.)
  Macmillan; New York; 2011, pp. 63–64.

2 See the criticism of "mind-emptying" prayer by
  both Popes John Paul II and Benedict XVI and
  the condemnation of "centering prayer" by many
  evangelical preachers, e.g., David Jeremiah, Gary
  Gilley, Christine Pack, Brent Barnett, Matt Slick, Chris
  Lawson, etc.

3 Matthew 6:33, *(my emphases).*

4 Mayne, Michael; *Prayer;* Darton, Longman & Todd;
  London; 2011, p. 4.

5 Malachi 3:6a.

6 Numbers 23:19.

7 *The Book of Common Prayer,* p. 133 *(my emphasis).*

8 Julian of Norwich (John-Julian, tr.) *Revelations of Divine
  Love,* Paraclete Press; Orleans, MA; 2011, Ch. 2.

9 Matthew 26:39.

10 *Revelations,* Ch. 41.

11 *Revelations,* Ch. 41.

12 *The Book of Common Prayer,* p. 331.

13 *Revelations,* Ch. 49.

14 *The Book of Common Prayer,* p. 393.

15 *Revelations,* Ch. 76.

16 1 John 4:12.

17 *The Book of Common Prayer*, p. 337 (*my emphases*).

18 Ibid. p. 230.

19 Cited in York; *A Faith Embracing All Creatures*; Wipf & Stock; Eugene, OR; 2012, p. 171.

20 *Revelations*, Ch. 4.

21 Monnin, Abbé Alfred; *Life of the Curé d'Ars*; Burns & Lambert; London; 1862, p. 57.

22 *The Fire of Your Life: A Solitude Shared*; Church Publishing; New York; 2007, p. 27.

23 *Revelations*, Ch. 41.

24 Ibid.

25 Bettelheim, Bruno; *The Uses of Enchantment: The Meaning and Importance of Fairy Tales*; Vintage Books/Knopf; New York; 1976.

26 *The Works of Cardinal Newman*; Longmans, Green & Co.; London; 1918, p. 43.

27 Exodus 14:14.

28 *The Book of Common Prayer*, p. 856.

29 *Passions*; Yale University Press.; New Haven, CT; 2014, p. 89.

30 *The Complete Cloud of Unknowing*; Paraclete Press; Orleans, MA; 2014, Ch. 5 *passim*.

31 *The Sacred Heart of the World*; Paulist Press; Mahwah, NJ; 2007, p. 58.

32 Romans 10:8.

33 S.M.C. (Anderson, Sister Mary Catherine, OP); *Brother Petroc's Return*; Little, Brown; Boston; 1946.

34 *Revelations*, Ch 27.

35 *Ibid.* Ch. 36.

36 *Ibid.* Ch. 13.

37 Please do not take this discussion to mean that I accept the personification of evil as "the Devil" or "Satan." I use these terms only because they are traditional ways of speaking of evil itself, and they appear often in the works of the mystics.

38 Glasscoe, Marion, ed.; *Julian of Norwich: A Revelation of Love*; University of Exeter Press; Exeter, UK; 1993, p. 38.

39 Gollancz; London; 1963.

40 Isaiah 55:8–9.

41 John 6:46.

42 Kavanaugh & Rodriguez; *The Collected Works of St. John of the Cross*; ICS Publications; Washington, DC; 1991.

43 The Acts of the Apostles 7:56.

44 *The Courage for Truth: The Letters of Thomas Merton to Writers*; Macmillan; New York; 1993, p. 124.

ABOUT PARACLETE PRESS

Who We Are

Paraclete Press is a publisher of books, recordings, and DVDs on Christian spirituality. Our publishing represents a full expression of Christian belief and practice—from Catholic to Evangelical, from Protestant to Orthodox.

We are the publishing arm of the Community of Jesus, an ecumenical monastic community in the Benedictine tradition. As such, we are uniquely positioned in the marketplace without connection to a large corporation and with informal relationships to many branches and denominations of faith.

What We Are Doing

PARACLETE PRESS BOOKS   Paraclete publishes books that show the richness and depth of what it means to be Christian. Although Benedictine spirituality is at the heart of all that we do, we publish books that reflect the Christian experience across many cultures, time periods, and houses of worship. We publish books that nourish the vibrant life of the church and its people.

We have several different series, including the best-selling Paraclete Essentials and Paraclete Giants series of classic texts in contemporary English; Voices from the Monastery—men and women monastics writing about living a spiritual life today; award-winning poetry; best-selling gift books for children on the occasions of baptism and first communion; and the Active Prayer Series that brings creativity and liveliness to any life of prayer.

MOUNT TABOR BOOKS   Paraclete's newest series, Mount Tabor Books, focuses on liturgical worship, art and art history, ecumenism, and the first millennium church, and was created in conjunction with the Mount Tabor Ecumenical Centre for Art and Spirituality in Barga, Italy.

PARACLETE RECORDINGS   From Gregorian chant to contemporary American choral works, our recordings celebrate the best of sacred choral music composed through the centuries that create a space for heaven and earth to intersect. Paraclete Recordings is the record label representing the internationally acclaimed choir Gloriæ Dei Cantores, praised for their "rapt and fathomless spiritual intensity" by *American Record Guide*; the Gloriæ Dei Cantores Schola, specializing in the study and performance of Gregorian chant; and the other instrumental artists of the Gloriæ Dei Artes Foundation.

Paraclete Press is also privileged to be the exclusive North American distributor of the recordings of the Monastic Choir of St. Peter's Abbey in Solesmes, France, long considered to be a leading authority on Gregorian chant.

PARACLETE VIDEO   Our DVDs offer spiritual help, healing, and biblical guidance for a broad range of life issues including grief and loss, marriage, forgiveness, facing death, bullying, addictions, Alzheimer's, and spiritual formation.

Learn more about us at our website:
www.paracletepress.com
or phone us toll-free at 1.800.451.5006

SCAN
TO
READ
MORE

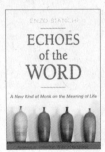